2 CDs

Accompaniments for Anthology of Spanish Song

High Voice

T0081533

Laura Ward, pianist

companion to this edition in The Vocal Library:
HL00740147 Anthology of Spanish Song, High Voice
edited by Maria DiPalma & Richard Walters

ISBN-13: 978-1-4234-1835-1
ISBN-10: 1-4234-1835-2

HAL•LEONARD®
CORPORATION
7777 W. BLUEMOUND RD. P.O. BOX 13819 MILWAUKEE, WI 53213

Visit Hal Leonard Online at
www.halleonard.com

In Australia Contact:
Hal Leonard Australia Pty. Ltd.
4 Lentara Court
Cheltenham, Victoria, 3192 Australia
Email: ausadmin@halleonard.com

Contents

Laura Ward, piano

DISC ONE Track List

Contents

Laura Ward, piano

DISC TWO Track List

About the Accompaniments

We've made every effort to choose a reasonable tempo for the recorded piano accompaniments, based on performance precedents. Other tempos could be explored for individual interpretations. We also deliberately attempted to make the accompaniment recordings musically alive, incorporating rubato, ritardandos, accelerandos, and dynamics to inspire a spirited performance. Nevertheless, by the very nature of recording, ours is only one interpretation.

Ideally, you will be using these recorded accompaniments for practice only. You will come up with a more individual interpretation, conjured from the ground up in the manner in which all the best artists work, if you learn the song on your own, built into your unique singing voice, without imitating a recorded performance.

We could have chosen technological options in recording these accompaniments, using MIDI or other devices. These were rejected on aesthetic grounds as being inappropriate to art music. The accompaniments were played on a Yamaha concert grand piano.

See the article "About the Enhanced CDs" for options in transpositions and changing tempos.

Richard Walters
Series Editor and Producer

About the Pianist

Laura Ward has recorded more piano accompaniments than any other pianist, with nearly 2000 tracks to her credit. Her recordings include twenty volumes in *The First Book of Solos* series (G. Schirmer), eight volumes of *Easy Songs for Beginning Singers* (G. Schirmer), *The First Book of Broadway Solos* series (four volumes, Hal Leonard), five volumes of *Standard Vocal Literature* (Hal Leonard, *The Vocal Library*), eleven other volumes in *The Vocal Library*, *The New Imperial Edition* (six volumes, Boosey & Hawkes), and various other collections. She has been a vocal coach and collaborative pianist at the Washington Opera, the Academy of Vocal Arts, the Ravinia Festival, the Music Academy of the West, the Blossom Festival, the University of Maryland, and Temple University. She is the official pianist for the Washington International Vocal competition and the Marian Anderson Award. She has performed at several international music festivals such as the Spoleto Festival in Spoleto, Italy and the Colmar International Music Festival and Saint Denis Festival in France. A native of Texas, Laura received her Bachelor of Music degree from Baylor University, Master of Music degree in Piano Accompanying at the Cincinnati College-Conservatory of Music and a Doctor of Musical Arts in Piano Accompanying from the University of Michigan with Martin Katz. There she was pianist for the Contemporary Directions Ensemble and she performed with the Ann Arbor Symphony. She is co-editor of *Richard Strauss: 40 Songs*, *Gabriel Fauré: 50 Songs*, and *Johannes Brahms*: *75 Songs*. She is co-founder and pianist for Lyric Fest, a dynamic and creative song series in Philadelphia.

About the Enhanced CDs

In addition to piano accompaniments playable on both your CD player and computer, these enhanced CDs also include tempo adjustment and transposition software for computer use only. This software, known as Amazing Slow Downer, was originally created for use in pop music to allow singers and players the freedom to independently adjust both tempo and pitch elements. Because we believe there may be valuable educational use for these features in classical and theatre music, we have included this software as a tool for both the teacher and student. For quick and easy installation instructions of this software, please see below.

In recording a piano accompaniment we necessarily must choose one tempo. Our choice of tempo, phrasing, ritardandos, and dynamics is carefully considered. But by the nature of recording, it is only one option.

However, we encourage you to explore your own interpretive ideas, which may differ from our recordings. This new software feature allows you to adjust the tempo up and down without affecting the pitch. Likewise, Amazing Slow Downer allows you to shift pitch up and down without affecting the tempo. We recommend that these new tempo and pitch adjustment features be used with care and insight. Ideally, you will be using these recorded accompaniments and Amazing Slow Downer for practice only.

The audio quality may be somewhat compromised when played through the Amazing Slow Downer. This compromise in quality will not be a factor in playing the CD audio track on a normal CD player or through another audio computer program.

INSTALLATION INSTRUCTIONS:

For Macintosh OS 8, 9 and X:
• Load the CD-ROM into your CD-ROM Drive on your computer.
• Each computer is set up a little differently. Your computer may automatically open the audio CD portion of this enhanced CD and begin to play it.
• To access the CD-ROM features, double-click on the data portion of the CD-ROM (which will have the Hal Leonard icon in red and be named as the book).
• Double-click on the "Amazing OS 8 (9 or X)" folder.
• Double-click "Amazing Slow Downer"/"Amazing X PA" to run the software from the CD-ROM, or copy this file to your hard disk and run it from there.
• Follow the instructions on-screen to get started. The Amazing Slow Downer should display tempo, pitch and mix bars. Click to select your track and adjust pitch or tempo by sliding the appropriate bar to the left or to the right.

For Windows:
• Load the CD-ROM into your CD-ROM Drive on your computer.
• Each computer is set up a little differently. Your computer may automatically open the audio CD portion of this enhanced CD and begin to play it.
• To access the CD-ROM features, click on My Computer then right click on the Drive that you placed the CD in. Click Open. You should then see a folder named "Amazing Slow Downer". Click to open the "Amazing Slow Downer" folder.
• Double-click "setup.exe" to install the software from the CD-ROM to your hard disk. Follow the on-screen instructions to complete installation.
• Go to "Start," "Programs" and find the "Amazing Slow Downer" folder. Go to that folder and select the "Amazing Slow Downer" software.
• Follow the instructions on-screen to get started. The Amazing Slow Downer should display tempo, pitch and mix bars. Click to select your track and adjust pitch or tempo by sliding the appropriate bar to the left or to the right.
• Note: On Windows NT, 2000 and XP, the user should be logged in as the "Administrator" to guarantee access to the CD-ROM drive. Please see the help file for further information.

MINIMUM SYSTEM REQUIREMENTS:

For Macintosh:
Power Macintosh; Mac OS 8.5 or higher; 4 MB Application RAM; 8x Multi-Session CD-ROM drive

For Windows:
Pentium, Celeron or equivalent processor; Windows 95, 98, ME, NT, 2000, XP; 4 MB Application RAM; 8x Multi-Session CD-ROM drive

Also available

The French Song Anthology
00740162 High Voice, book only
00000453 High Voice, accompaniment CDs
00740163 Low Voice, book only
00000454 Low Voice, accompaniment CDs

Contents

HECTOR BERLIOZ
Villanelle

GEORGES BIZET
Chanson d'avril
Guitare
Ouvre ton cœur

EMMANUEL CHABRIER
Les cigales
Villanelle des petits canards

ERNEST CHAUSSON
Hébé
Le charme
Le colibri
Le temps des lilas

CLAUDE DEBUSSY
Beau soir
Les cloches
Mandoline
Noël des enfants qui n'ont plus de maisons

HENRI DUPARC
Chanson triste
La vie antérieure
Lamento

GABRIEL FAURÉ
Après un rêve
Automne
Chanson d'amour
Clair de lune
Lydia
Mandoline
Notre amour

CÉSAR FRANCK
Nocturne

CHARLES GOUNOD
L'absent
O ma belle rebelle
Venise

REYNALDO HAHN
À Chloris
Offrande
Si mes vers avaient des ailes

VINCENT D'INDY
Madrigal

CHARLES KOECHLIN
Si tu le veux

FRANZ LISZT
Oh! quand je dors

JOHANN-PAUL MARTINI
Plaisir d'amour

JULES MASSENET
Nuit d'Espagne
Si tu veux, Mignonne

WOLFGANG AMADEUS MOZART
Dans un bois solitaire

EMILE PALADILHE
Psyché

FRANCIS POULENC
Le Bestiaire:
Le dromadaire
La chèvre du Thibet
La sauterelle
Le dauphin
L'écrevisse
La carpe

MAURICE RAVEL
Sainte

Cinq mélodies populaires grecques:
Le réveil de la mariée
Là-bas, vers l'église
Quel galant m'est comparable?
Chanson des cueilleuses de lentisques
Tout gai!

ALBERT ROUSSEL
Le bachelier de Salamanque
Sarabande

CAMILLE SAINT-SAËNS
Aimons-nous
L'attente

ERIK SATIE
Je te veux
La statue de bronze

DÉODAT DE SÉVERAC
Les hiboux
Philis

PAULINE VIARDOT
Fleur desséchée

Also available

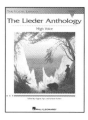

The Lieder Anthology

00740219 High Voice, book only
00000455 High Voice, accompaniment CDs
00740220 Low Voice, book only
00000456 Low Voice, accompaniment CDs

Contents

LUDWIG VAN BEETHOVEN
Der Kuß
Ich liebe dich
Sehnsucht

JOHANNES BRAHMS
Dein blaues Auge
Die Mainacht
Immer leiser wird mein Schlummer
Meine Liebe ist grün
Sonntag
Ständchen
Vergebliches Ständchen
Wie Melodien zieht es mir

Ophelia Lieder
    Wie erkenn ich dein Treulieb
    Sein Leichenhemd weiss
    Auf morgen ist Sankt Valentins Tag
    Sie trugen ihn auf der Bahre bloss
    Und kommt er nicht mehr zurück?

ROBERT FRANZ
Aus meinen großen Schmerzen
Er ist gekommen
Für Musik
Im Herbst

GUSTAV MAHLER
Frühlingsmorgen
Liebst du um Schönheit
Lob des hohen Verstandes
Wer hat dies Liedlein erdacht?

ALMA SCHINDLER MAHLER
Laue Sommernacht

FANNY MENDELSSOHN HENSEL
Italien

FELIX MENDELSSOHN
Der Blumenstrauß
Neue Liebe

WOLFGANG AMADEUS MOZART
Abendempfindung
Als Luise die Briefe ihres ungetreuen
    Liebhabers verbrannte
Das Veilchen

FRANZ SCHUBERT
An die Musik
Auf dem Wasser zu singen
Der Musensohn
Die Forelle
Du bist die Ruh
Gretchen am Spinnrade
Lachen und Weinen
Nacht und Träume
Rastlose Liebe
Ständchen (from *Schwanengesang*)

CLARA WIECK SCHUMANN
Liebst du um Schönheit

ROBERT SCHUMANN
Der Nußbaum
Die Lotosblume
Du bist wie eine Blume
Du Ring an meinen Finger
Ich grolle nicht
In der Fremde
Intermezzo
Waldesgespräch
Widmung

RICHARD STRAUSS
Allerseelen
Breit' über mein Haupt
Die Nacht
Du meines Herzens Krönelein
Ich trage meine Minne
Morgen!
Zueignung

HUGO WOLF
Anakreons Grab
Auch kleine Dinge
Auf ein altes Bild
Der Musikant
In dem Schatten meiner Locken
Lebe wohl
Verborgenheit